I0461303

How Many Is God?

How Many Is God?

Rev. William H. Carey

Lighthouse

Contents

**Rev. William H.
Carey**

About the Author

A native of Brooklyn, NY, Brother Carey attended high school in Galway, NY, college and ministerial training in Schenectady, and has ministered in that city, as well as in Nebraska, Texas and Michigan. He is co-founder and past Presbyter of Apostolic Restoration Mission. His studies in Greek began at the age of 12, and in Hebrew at the age of 19.

Brother Carey is also the author of **The Basics of New Testament Teaching: An Apostolic Guide to Doctrine** and has published a modern English translation of the New Testament.

This work is gratefully dedicated to Bro. Tom B., who had the courage to tell a fifteen year old boy that God is One. I was that boy, and I've never forgotten.

Copyright © 2022 by Lighthouse

All rights reserved. No part of this book may be reproduced in any manner whatsoever without written permission except in the case of brief quotations embodied in critical articles and reviews.

First Printing, 2022

Prologue

"What *do* you believe, then?"

This is the question I am most often asked when I mention that I don't believe in the Trinity. One Christian minister, a dedicated man of God, even declared that I could not be a fundamentalist Christian if I did not believe in the doctrine of the Trinity.

So what *do* I believe? Do I deny the deity of Jesus Christ? Never! Do I disbelieve the existence of the Father or the Holy Ghost? Not at all! Then what exactly is my teaching? It is called **Oneness**. Throughout Christian history, it has been called many other names by well-meaning people who didn't understand it. Names such as *Sabellianism* (after Bishop Sabellius, an early Oneness believer), *Modalism*, and "*Jesus Only*" have been assigned to the doctrine of the Oneness of God. Much has been written against this teaching, and yet, upon reading these anti-Oneness writings, it is clear that the authors did not understand the doctrine, and were basing their works on what they *thought* Oneness was.

I once heard a minister decry the Oneness doctrine from his pulpit, telling his flock to beware "those Oneness people, who won't let Jesus have a Daddy." Does Oneness teach that Jesus had no Father? No, it doesn't.

I have often been asked to explain what I believe. A surprising number of people, upon hearing what Oneness teaches, have responded by saying, "But that's what *I* believe!" My answer to them is this: "Then you are not a Trinitarian."

An even greater number of self-professed Trinitarians express belief in a doctrine that falls somewhere between Trinitarianism and Oneness. The truth is, believers in actual Trinitarianism seem to be a small minority. For this reason, I have chosen to begin this writing with a section on the Trinity and orthodox Trinitarian belief. Before doing so, I would like to make the following statement regarding Trinitarians:

Trinitarian Christians are my sisters and brothers. I love and respect them, and will worship with them if welcomed to do so. I stand always ready to explain Oneness to any of them, but will not attempt to force my beliefs on anyone. I will not judge anyone, nor do I believe that a person must believe in Oneness to be saved. I do not have the right, nor does any Christian, Oneness or Trinitarian, to decide who will and who will not be saved. In the words of John, *"Let us love one another..."* and leave the judgment to God.

{ 2 }

What is the Trinity?

What is the Trinity, and who is Trinitarian? Throughout this writing, I will be using the term "orthodox Trinitarianism." This refers to the doctrine of the Trinity as it is laid out in the early creeds, and as it is accepted by nearly every Christian denomination. This is in contrast to a "nominal Trinitarianism," believers who consider themselves Trinitarian, but whose actual concept of the Godhead is not Trinitarian in the orthodox sense. Nominal Trinitarians may range anywhere from an untaught knowledge of Oneness to a hybrid Trinitarianism to a pure Unitarianism. (Note: Oneness and Unitarianism are *not* the same. Unitarianism teaches that Jesus is not God.) Some nominal Trinitarians have no clear concept of the Godhead at all, and call themselves Trinitarian simply because their churches use the word Trinity.

Early Trinitarian writings include the Nicene Creed (Council of Nicea, 325 AD) and the *Quicumque Vult* (Latin: "Whoever wants"). Also known as the Athanasian Creed, the *Quicumque Vult* was probably written somewhere between 325 and 500 AD.

The Council of Nicea was the first serious attempt to make the Trinitarian concept of the Godhead "official" church teaching. Those of opposing viewpoints, including the Oneness Bishops, refused to accept the resulting creed, and were excommunicated. Oddly enough, while the Nicene Creed *enforced* Trinitarian belief, it did little to *explain* the doctrine of the Trinity.

Orthodox Trinitarianism teaches that the Godhead is an incomprehensible mystery. It goes on to explain that there is one God who eternally exists in three Persons. These Persons are separate, co-eternal, co-equal and co-existent.

This doctrine necessitates the existence of three thrones in heaven, since the Godhead is made up of three Persons.[1] The terms God the Father, God the Son, and God the Holy Spirit (or Holy Ghost) are used to describe the three. (Although the phrase "God the Father" is found in scripture, neither "God the Son" nor "God the Holy Spirit" is found there.) While this "three individuals on three thrones" may not reflect the beliefs of some readers, it is nonetheless orthodox Trinitarianism, and is the accepted belief of the vast majority of Christian churches.

Below is the text of the Nicene Creed, first in the original Greek, then in English translation. I have numbered the lines for ease of reference.

1. Πιστεύομεν εἰς ἕνα Θεόν.
2. Πατέρα, παντοκράτορα,
3. πάντων ὁρατῶν τε καὶ ἀοράτων ποιητήν.
4. Καὶ εἰς ενα Κύριον Ἰησοῦν Χριστόν,
5. τὸν Υἱὸν τοῦ Θεοῦ,
6. γεννηθέντα ἐκ τοῦ Πατρὸς μονογενῆ,
7. τουτέστιν ἐκ τῆς οὐσίας τοῦ Πατρός,
8. Θεὸν ἐκ Θεοῦ, Φῶς ἐκ Φωτός,
1. Θεὸν ἀληθινὸν ἐκ Θεοῦ ἀληθινοῦ,
2. γεννηθέντα οὐ ποιηθέντα,
3. ὁμοούσιον τῷ Πατρί,
4. δὶ οὗ τὰ πάντα ἐγένετο,
5. τά τε ἐν τῷ οὐρανῷ καὶ τὰ ἐν τῇ γῇ,
6. τὸν δὶ ἡμᾶς τοὺς ἀνθρώπους

7. καὶ διὰ τὴν ἡμετέραν σωτηρίαν,
8. κατελθόντα καὶ σαρκωθέντα,
9. ἐνανθρωπήσαντα, παθόντα
10. καὶ ἀναστάντα τῇ τρίτῃ ἡμέρᾳ,
11. ἀνελθόντα εἰς οὐρανούς,
12. ἐρχόμενον κρῖναι ζῶντας καὶ νεκρούς.
13. Καὶ εἰς τὸ Ἅγιου Πνεῦμα.
14. Τοὺς δὲ λέγοντας ἦν ποτε ὅτε οὐκ ἦν,

καὶ πρὶν γεννηθῆναι οὐκ ἦν, καὶ ὅτι ἐξ οὐκ ὄντων ἐγένετο, ἢ ἐξ ἑτέρας ὑποστάσεως ἢ οὐσίας φάσκοντας εἶναι, ἢ τρεπτὸν ἢ ἀλλοιωτὸν τὸν Υἱὸν τοῦ Θεοῦ, ἀναθεματίζει ἡ καθολικὴ καὶ ἀποστολικὴ ἐκκλησία.

1. We believe in one God,
2. Father almighty,
3. Maker of all things visible and invisible.
4. And in one Lord, Jesus Christ,
5. the Son of God,
6. the only son born of the Father
7. that is, from the substance of the Father:
8. God from God, Light from Light,
9. True God from True God,
10. Born, not made,
11. of the same substance as the Father,
12. through whom all things were born,
13. both in heaven and on earth.
14. Because of us men
15. and for the sake of our salvation,
16. came down and took on flesh,
17. became man, suffered,

18. and rose up on the third day,
19. ascended into heaven,
20. and will come to judge the living and the dead.
21. And in the Holy Spirit.
22. The Catholic and apostolic church will surely anathematize (curse) anyone who asserts that there was a time when He (i.e., Christ) wasn't, and that before He was born, He was not, or that He was not truly born, or that He is not of the same substance or being as the Creator, or that He is changeable, or that He is other than the Son of God.[2]

Now here is part of the text of the *Quicumque Vult*, first in the original Latin, then in English translation. Once again, the lines have been numbered for the purpose of reference.

1. *Quicumque vult salvus esse: Ante omnia opus est ut teneat Catholicam fidem,*
2. *quam nisi quis integram inviolatamque servaverit: absque dubio in æternum peribit.*
3. *Fides autem Catholica hæc est: Ut unum Deum in trinitate et Trinitatem in unitate veneremur,*
4. *neque confundentes personas, neque substantiam separantes;*
5. *alia est enim persona Patris, alia Filii, alia Spiritus Sancti;*
6. *Sed Patris et Filii et Spiritus Sancti una est divinitas: æqualis gloria, coæterna majestas...*
7. *Ita Deus Pater, Deus Filius, Deus Spiritus Sanctus;*
8. *et tamen non tres dii, sed unus Deus;*
1. *Ita Dominus Pater, Dominus Filius, Dominus Spiritus Sanctus;*
2. *et tamen non tres domini, ded unus Dominus.*
3. *Quia sicut singillatim unamquamque Personam et Deum et Dominum confiteri, Christiana veritate compellimur,*

4. *ita tres deos aut tres dominos dicere, Catholica religione prohibemur.*

5. *Pater a nullo est factus, nec creatus, nec genitus;*

6. *Filius a Patre solo est; non factus, nec creatus, sed genitus;*

7. *Spiritus Sanctus a Patre et Filio; non factus, nec creatus, nec genitus, sed procedens.*

8. *Unus ergo Pater, non tres patres; unus Filius, non tres filii; unus Spiritus Sanctus, non tres spiritus sancti.*

9. *In hac Trinitate nihil prius aut posterius; nihil majus aut minus, sed totæ tres Personæ coæternæ sibi sunt, et coæquales.*

10. *Ita ut per omnia, sicut jam supra dictum est, et Trinitas in Unitate et Unitas in Trinitate veneranda sit.*

11. *Qui vult ergo salvus esse, ita de Trinitate sentiat...*

12. *Hæc est fides Catholica, quam nisi quis fideliter firmiterque crediderit, salvus esse non poterit.*

1. Whoever wants to be saved, before all needs to hold the Catholic faith,

2. which, unless one keeps it wholly and inviolately, without doubt he will perish in eternity.

3. Now this is the Catholic faith: That we worship one God in Trinity, and the Trinity in unity,

4. neither confusing the Persons, nor dividing the substance.

5. There is one Person of the Father, another of the Son, another of the Holy Spirit.

6. But the divinity of the Father and of the Son and of the Holy Spirit is one: equal Glory, co-eternal majesty...

7. Thus, the Father is God, the Son is God, the Holy Spirit is God,

8. and yet there are not three gods, but one God.

9. Thus, the Father is Lord, the Son is Lord, the Holy Spirit is Lord,

10. and yet there are not three lords, but one Lord.

11. For as Christian truth compels us to acknowledge singly each Person and God and Lord,

12. thus the Catholic religion forbids us to say three gods or three lords.
13. The Father is made by no one, neither created nor begotten.
14. The Son is only from the Father, not made or created, but begotten.
1. The Holy Spirit is from the Father and the Son, not made or created or begotten, but proceeding forth.
2. Therefore there is one Father, not three fathers; one Son, not three sons; one Holy Spirit, not three holy spirits.
3. In this Trinity, none is before or after, none is greater or lesser, but all three Persons are co-eternal and co-equal.
4. Thus through all, as already mentioned above, both Trinity in unity and unity in Trinity are to be worshipped.
5. Who wants to be saved must perceive the Trinity thus...
6. This is the Catholic faith, which, unless one believes faithfully and firmly, he will not be able to be saved.

It can be seen that the Athanasian Creed is far more explicit in its definition of the Trinity than Nicea was. The reason for this may have been the failure of Nicea to fully define the teaching it declared an essential part of Christianity.

Both Creeds proclaim that God is one (Nicea, Line 1; Athanasius, Line 3). Athanasius declares that God is three Persons (Line 5) and that all three are equal and co-eternal (Lines 6, 17). Nicea threatens non-Trinitarians with being cursed by the church, while Athanasius claims that belief in the Trinity is paramount both to Christianity and salvation.

Early Oneness believers accused the Trinitarians of tritheism, that is, belief in three gods. Naturally, the accusation was denied, and both creeds do state that God is one. But let us look more closely at Athanasius:

Line 7 declares that the Father is God, the Son is God and the Holy Spirit is God.

Line 8 says that there are not three gods, but one.

Line 9 says that the Father is Lord, the Son is Lord and the Holy Spirit is Lord.

Line 10 says that there are not three lords, but one.

But now, look at lines 11 and 12: **"For as Christian truth compels us to acknowledge singly each Person and God and Lord, thus the Catholic religion forbids us to say three gods or three lords."** Let's re-state that in plainer English: "Christian truth forces us to *acknowledge* individually each Person, **each God**, and each Lord, but the Catholic religion forbids us to *say* that they are three Gods or three Lords." (In other words, we *believe* in three Gods, but we're not allowed to *admit* it!)

Some will say at this point that neither creed should be the basis of doctrine, but rather the scripture should decide. And this writer agrees. Let's take the Trinity to the Bible, and see what happens.

We have our three Persons: The Father, the Son, and the Holy Ghost. We can all agree that Jesus is the Son. But which of the remaining two Persons is the Father of Jesus? Trinitarian teaching says that the Person "God the Father" is the Father of Jesus. What does the Bible say? According to Matthew 1:18, 20, Mary became pregnant **by the Holy Ghost**, which would make the Holy Ghost the Father of Jesus. This leaves us with only two possibilities: Either the Persons we're calling Father and Holy Ghost are one and the same Person, or Jesus was calling the wrong one Father!

Is it possible that the Father and the Holy Spirit are the same Person? Jesus told us that God is a Spirit (singular) *(John 4:24)*. Ephesians 4:4 says that there is only one Spirit. Because there is no other Spirit, God the Father **must** be the Holy Spirit. (The Jews also understood their God to be a Spirit, and understood David's reference to the Holy Spirit in Ps. 51:11 to mean God Himself.)

In Matthew 28:18, Jesus declared that **all** power in heaven and earth was now His. But where did that leave the Father and Holy Ghost? If there are three Persons in the Godhead, two of them were now without any power. A person without any power cannot be God.

Athanasius line 4 warned us against "confusing the Persons." And yet, by simply looking at a few verses of scripture, the "Persons" are very confused! Isaiah 9:6 will confuse them even further, because Isaiah said that the Son (Jesus) would be called the "everlasting Father." Jesus told Phillip and the other disciples that by seeing Him, that had **already** seen the Father. (John 14:9)

But Athanasius said not to confuse the Persons... But once we open the scripture, the Trinitarian doctrine gets very confusing, and it becomes impossible to tell whether God is one, two, three, or more. No wonder they just say "It's a mystery!" Incidentally, ancient Babylon also worshipped a trinitarian godhead, which they couldn't explain either. They called it a mystery, and "mystery" became their explanation for any doctrine they couldn't explain. The Roman church adopted the same explanation for many of their doctrines,

including the Trinity.

The prophet Isaiah found himself standing before the throne of God *(Is. 6:1)*. Only one throne was there, and only one Person sat on it. Where were the other two Persons?

The apostle John also found himself standing before God's throne *(Rev. 4:2)*. Again, only one throne, and One sitting on it. Where were the other two? Some would say that the lamb in Rev. 5:6 was Jesus. While the lamb may have *symbolized* Jesus, Jesus is no more a slain lamb than the Holy Ghost is a bird! The only real God was sitting on the throne.

With my apologies to Athanasius, it is not possible to avoid confusing the Persons of the Trinity, if one considers them separate Persons as the doctrine teaches. The orthodox Trinity falls apart, or more accurately, merges into one Person, each time we open the Bible. And one Person in the Godhead is *not* Trinitarianism; it's Oneness!

{ 3 }

What is the Doctrine of Oneness?

There is one God. *(Deut. 6:4; Mk. 12:29; James 2:19)*

God is a Spirit. *(John 4:24)*

This one Spirit, (known as *Jehovah* or *Yahweh*)³ caused Mary to conceive. *(Mt. 1:18, 20)*

From the physical perspective, the resulting baby was the son of God, since the Spirit Jehovah was his Father.

The Spirit then inhabited this body for the purpose of our salvation. *(2 Cor. 5:19)*

The child was named Jesus.⁴

The son could rightly be called the Father *(Is. 9:6)*, because the Father, that is God, the one Spirit, was **in** the son, that is, in the flesh. The "son" refers only to the physical body of Jesus. The son is not a "Person" in the Godhead, and did not exist until Mary conceived him. (Trinitarian teaching maintains that the Son always existed.) Ps. 2:7 and Hebrews 1:5 teach us that the son did indeed have a beginning.

Jesus was *Immanuel,* that is, "God with us," because **all** the fullness of the Godhead was in Him *(Col. 2:9)*.

From His mother, Jesus inherited a human body and a human nature. As a human, he felt hunger, thirst, pain and fear. He prayed and cried as a man. But the Spirit of God also inhabited that body.

As God, He forgave sins, healed the sick and raised the dead. Did God die on the cross? No. By definition, God is immortal and cannot die. It was the son, the flesh, the man Jesus who died. By becoming the sacrifice, Jesus became sin for us *(2 Cor. 5:21)*. In so doing, he took upon himself all sins that were ever committed. The Spirit of God would not remain in the presence of sin, and withdrew from Jesus *(Mt. 27:46; Mk. 15:34)*. Thus, only the man, the son, remained on the cross and died. The Spirit and flesh were reunited following the resurrection *(Jn. 20:17)*.

In Trinitarian theology, the Jehovah of the Old Testament is often understood to be God the Father. With this thought in mind, let us make some comparisons, and draw some conclusions:

- Is. 44:24 and 45:18 say that **Jehovah** created the heavens and the earth. John 1:3 says that **Jesus** created everything.
- Is. 43:11 says that **Jehovah** is the only Savior. Mt. 1:21 says that **Jesus** will save us.
- Is. 44:6 says that **Jehovah** is the First and the Last. Rev. 1:11, 17, 18 and 22:13 say that **Jesus** is the First and the Last. Can there be *two* Firsts and Lasts?
- Is. 54:5 says that **Jehovah** is our Husband. Rev. 21:9 says that we are the Bride of the Lamb, that is, **Jesus**.

We believe that the Bible does not contradict itself. Therefore, we have no choice but to admit that the Jesus of the New Testament **is** the Jehovah of the Old Testament.

{ 4 }

Some Questions

Isn't the Godhead a mystery? 1 Tim. 3:16 calls it a mystery, but the same verse reveals the mystery, so that it's a mystery no more: "...God was manifest (i.e., shown or revealed) in the flesh..." 2 Cor. 5:19 says it again: "...God was *in* Christ...."

Doesn't Matthew 28:19 prove that God is three Persons?

Does it? What does the previous verse say? Jesus said that *all* power was given to Him, and went on to say in v. 19 "Go ye therefore (that is, *because* I have all power)... baptizing them in the name of the Father and of the Son and of the Holy Ghost...." So Jesus said that because He had all power, we were to baptize all nations in the name of the Father and of the Son and of the Holy Ghost. And I ask you, what *is* the NAME of the Father and of the Son and of the Holy Ghost? Father, Son and Holy Ghost are not names, but titles. And the word "name" in verse 19 is singular, indicating that there is one name that applies to all three titles. There's no question that the Son's name is Jesus *(Mt. 1:21)*. But what is the Father's name? Is it just God? No, that's also a title. Is it Jehovah? It *was*, in the Old Testament. But the name "Jesus" *contains* the name "Jehovah." Jesus, as a man, said, "I have come in my Father's name..." *(Jn. 5:43)*. The Greek preposition translated "in" implies "using." So if the name that Jesus was using as His own was the Father's, then the name "Jesus" must apply to the Father as well as the son. In prayer, Jesus said, "I have manifested (that is, shown or revealed) thy name..." *(Jn. 17:6)*. The only name He manifested was "Jesus." And logically, a son should bear his Father's name.

What about the Holy Ghost? Does the Holy Ghost have a name? Jn. 14:26 tells us that the Holy Ghost also comes *in* (using) the name of Jesus. Therefore, the name of the Father, Son and Holy Ghost is Jesus. Want further proof? Look how the command of Mt. 28:19 was carried out by the Apostles: Not once did they repeat the titles Father, Son and Holy Ghost in baptism. In every case, they baptized their converts, Jews, Samaritans and Gentiles, in the name of Jesus *(Acts 2:38; 8:16; 10:48; 19:5)*. Did they disobey the command of Mt. 28:19, or did they understand something that has eluded the church since the fourth century, that Jesus **is** the name of the Father, Son and Holy Ghost?[5]

What about 1 John 5:7? If you are using a King James Version, your Bible contains this verse: *"for there are three that bear record in heaven, the Father, the Word, and the Holy Ghost, and these three are one."* I invite you to look up the same verse in the New International Version. It isn't there. Why not? The verse is found only in a footnote, explaining that it first appeared in late manuscripts of the Latin Vulgate. It does not appear in **any** of the ancient Greek manuscripts.[6] There is not even a shadow of a doubt that this verse was not part of the original epistle, but was added centuries later. It is without scriptural authority. Why was it added? Probably because someone realized that the scriptures would not support the teaching of a three-Person Godhead. In 1611 AD, the translators of the King James Versions had access to many ancient Greek manuscripts, but didn't avail themselves of them, choosing instead to use newer manuscripts, focusing primarily on the flawed *Textus Receptus*, which was only about one hundred years old, and which had been altered to agree with late versions of the Latin Vulgate. They chose to include it for the same reason it was added in the first place: They knew that without it, the scriptures could not support the Trinitarian teaching of their church.

"Let us make man in our image..." *(Gen. 1:26)*. **Doesn't this prove more than one Person?** If so, why, then, do the pronouns return to the singular in the very next verse? *"...in H<u>is</u> own image created H<u>e</u> him... created H<u>e</u> them."* Speaking with the "royal we" no more proves that God is three, than it proved that Queen Victoria was three when she said, "We are not amused." Deut. 6:4, translated directly from Hebrew, has this to say: "Hear, O Israel: YHVH (i.e., Jehovah) is our God; YHVH is ONE." (In contrast to the Babylonian religion, which was already worshipping a three-person god when Deuteronomy was written.

What about John 1:1? Doesn't it say that Jesus (the Word) was *with* God in the beginning? The first chapter of John's Gospel contains a very powerful proof of Oneness. Unfortunately, those who translated the Bible into English (every commonly available English translation) hid that proof by mistranslating the first two verses of this chapter. The phrase ἦν πρὸς τὸν Θεόν, which they translated as "was with God" literally translates as "was toward God." Idiomatically, it means "was pertaining to God."[7] The first two verses of John's Gospel should read "In the beginning was the Word, and the Word pertained to God (i.e., *meant* God), and the Word was God. This pertained to *(meant)* God in the beginning."

But what is the Word? To find the answer, we have to go back to the Aramaic translation of the Old Testament. Following the Jewish people's captivity in Babylon, Hebrew ceased to be their spoken language. Instead, Aramaic, a closely related language, took its place. Aramaic was the spoken language of Jesus and His apostles, and they wrote it using the Hebrew alphabet.[8]

In order to facilitate study of the Jewish scriptures, an Aramaic translation had been made. The translators felt, however, that God's name (יהוה, YHVH, Jehovah) was too holy to be written in any language other than Hebrew. (Hebrew is known as *l'shon hakodesh*, the holy tongue.) Therefore, the translators needed a way to represent the name without actually writing it. Throughout their translation, they replaced the holy name with the Aramaic word ממרא *memra*. It means *word*. Readers coming across it would understand that it stood for God's name, much the same as many English Bibles have replaced the name with the word **LORD** in all capital letters.

John wrote his Gospel in Greek, which was the language of culture in his day. Being a devout Jew, writing to devout Jews, he reasoned that if God's name were too holy to be written in Aramaic, a language related to Hebrew and even using the same alphabet, then it was certainly far too holy to write in a "pagan" tongue like Greek. He needed a way to let

his readers know that he was talking about Jehovah without writing that name.[9] He took a cue from the Aramaic, and used the word *Word*. The Greek equivalent was λόγος (*Logos*).

Of course, having this "codeword" wasn't of any use if his readers didn't know what it meant. So his first two sentences defined it for them: "In the beginning was *Logos*, and *Logos* meant God, and *Logos* was God. This meant God in the beginning." By these two sentences, his readers would understand that *Logos* was being used as a synonym for God. And a reader familiar with the Aramaic Old Testament would understand immediately that *Logos* meant *Jehovah*.

With this understanding, that the *Word* means *Jehovah*, let's read verse 14: "The Word (*Jehovah*) was made flesh." "...God was manifest in the flesh..."(*1 Tim. 3:16*). This is the doctrine of Oneness.

Perhaps the reader has questions, or wishes to study the matter further. I would recommend the following books, which will be very helpful in understanding this subject:

Endnotes

1. ^In medieval art, the Trinity was often depicted as three Persons on thrones. Sometimes this took the form of three individuals of like appearance, and other times, as an older man, a younger man, and a dove.

2. ^It was necessary to change the word order of the anathema in order to translate it into English, making a line by line translation impossible. Therefore, the number 22 is assigned to the entire anathema.

3. ^

    Hebrew: יהוה YHVH; Exodus 6:3

4. ^Original Hebrew: יהושע Yehoshua, a name formed by taking part of יהוה YHVH [Jehovah] and combining it with part of the word ישועה yeshua, which means salvation. (This is, coincidentally, also the modern Hebrew pronunciation of Jesus.) The resulting name implies that "Jehovah has become salvation." See Is. 12:2.

5. ^

    Church history confirms that the first century church always baptized in Jesus' name. It was not until the fourth century that repeating the titles of Mt. 28:19 became universal.

6. ^The earliest Greek manuscript containing this verse is from the eleventh century, and it was not in the text, but scrawled in the margin. It wasn't until the sixteenth century that it appeared in the actual text of a Greek manuscript.

7. ^In Hebrews 2:17, the exact same Greek idiom is correctly translated as "pertaining to God."
8. ^The Jewish people still write Aramaic with the Hebrew alphabet, although the churches and people that use the language today have three scripts they use, closer to Arabic than Hebrew.
9. ^There really wasn't much choice anyway. The Greek alphabet lacks the necessary letters to represent the four consonants.

www.ingramcontent.com/pod-product-compliance
Lightning Source LLC
Chambersburg PA
CBHW060359130626
46553CB00003B/1301

* 9 7 9 8 9 8 5 8 4 9 1 4 1 *